"This book is funny and smart. I always knew you could write!"

—Mildred Alvino, My grandmother

"There's a Hot Mom inside each of us and it's possible to find 'her' with *The Hot Mom's Handbook*. Kudos to Jessica Denay for standing up against society's beliefs on motherhood and encouraging moms to realize that their lives did not end when they became a mother. Denay's writing inspires all mothers to be proud of the one title that can never be taken away."

—Victoria Pericon (a.k.a. Savvy Mommy), Family
Lifestyle Expert, Author of *Mommy Land*

"The book looks great, Jess! I am so proud of you!"

—Gail Lahm, My mom

"The Hot Moms Club is all about confidence and knowing who you are! I love it!"

—Natasha Henstridge, Actress

THE HOT MOM'S
HANDBOOK

~~BLONDES~~ *Moms* HAVE MORE FUN!

THE HOT MOM'S HANDBOOK

Moms
~~BLONDES~~ HAVE MORE FUN!

Jessica Denay

NAKED INK

Published in Nashville, Tennessee by NAKED INK™ of the General Trade Book Group of Thomas Nelson Publishers. Please visit us at www.nakedink.net.

Grateful acknowledgement is made to all of the Hot Moms who contributed to this book. All quotes used by permission.

NAKED INK books may be purchased in bulk for educational, business, fundraising, or sales promotional use. For more information please e-mail SpecialMarkets@ThomasNelson.com.

Library of Congress cataloging-in-publication data on file with the Library of Congress.

ISBN 1595558519
Printed in the United States of America
06 07 08 09 10 – 5 4 3 2 1

THIS BOOK BELONGS TO

HOT MOM

DEDICATION

For my Mom
for teaching me to always keep a sense of humor,
for indulging my visions and
never putting a ceiling on my sky.

For my son Gabriel
for opening up a new dimension
of love in my heart
and being.

CONTENTS

Growing up, adults were always telling me, "If only I knew when I was your age what I know now." Most of the time when I heard this, my response was one of indifference. Interesting that I now find myself making the same proclamation to those younger than me! There is, however, always the silent thought that accompanies my admonishment, "I would not smooth out a single bump in my life's road. All that jostling made me...me."

I was thirty-eight when I became a mom for the first time. (Older by many people's standards, younger by other's.) I now have three sons. Azer (Alexander) is four, George is three, and Henry is two. I became a mom at the right time for me. I knew that our relationship would and could be one of mutual enrichment, albeit a noisy one!

Instinctually I keep them safe, nurture them and prepare them for their future. I am a mom! But, my boys do the same for me. They remind me constantly that they love *me*, not just the old-fashioned definition of what a "mother" is and does.

Azer loves my traditions and his memory of details is astounding. He loves the repetition that traditions bring, and for me, I have the comfort of knowing I'll leave a legacy. He especially loves my silly traditions like their birthdays which are always exciting, but I thought mom's

birthday should be exciting too. No, I don't have hats and noisemakers, but I do have two cakes. The second cake is just for fun. The boys strip down and we have a cake fight. The first year this occurred in the dining room. We've since moved it outside! Mom's birthday has become a tradition we look forward to all year.

George loves beauty. He seems so proud when I dress up and he loves to make anything a special occasion. We plan special dinners where we all dress up and wear our "fancy" shoes. Mom and Dad have wine and the boys have shirley temples. The way he looks at me when I'm dressed up stays with me for days. He also loves touch. We all give lots of kisses and hugs, and take turns giving massages. Lucky for me, they always get Daddy to join in. They are so happy when Mommy and Daddy have their own kisses and hugs, as are we.

Henry loves being silly, which is wonderful as I love being silly too! I love to blast the stereo and dance any way I want to. So does he. We often dance and dance until we're sweaty. It doesn't matter what stresses are going on in my day, crazy dancing melts them away. All the boys join in and a good night's sleep is all that's on the agenda!

Ultimately, children learn by example. They do what they see. My boys see that I take my job seriously and work very hard. They see that I try to take care of myself. I eat healthy meals, exercise, get plenty of sleep (!), and am loving and affectionate. I talk about things and listen to what is being said. And just because Mommy and Daddy sometimes need "private time," my boys like their own private time too. And just as Mommy makes sure to love herself as well as her sons, my boys' self-esteem grows and grows as they learn to love themselves as well as others. So at the risk of sounding repetitive, take what I know now and apply it, no matter what your age. You too can be a Hot Mom!

—Lauren Holly

PREFACE

The Hot Moms Club is a community of empowered, confident mothers of all ages and all walks of life who are committed to boldly redefining motherhood.

I haven't always been a Hot Mom. The "Hot Mom" movement was actually born out of my insecurities as a single mom and my need to feel whole. I couldn't have written this book four years ago, three years ago, even two years ago. In many ways I am *still* discovering everyday what a Hot Mom is...it's a journey.

In this handbook I am going to share with you the secrets and exercises that have changed my life forever! I have outlined steps to revealing your Hot Mom spirit and have tossed all those old "mommy myths" *right out the minivan window!*

If you let it, this can be an awakening experience. The messages and real-life stories found here will help you connect or reconnect with your true self, and encourage you NOT to abandon your identity but to embrace it and become a Hot Mom! And just who is a Hot Mom? Not what you might think. It's simply an attitude and a way of being.

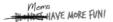

A Hot Mom can be eighteen or ninety-eight, a size two or a size twenty-two, have one child or fifteen! A Hot Mom can wear a business suit, or ride motorcycles. A Hot Mom can have a nose ring and tattoos, or wear aprons and bake cookies with love (or both!). A Hot Mom knows no shape, size, or situation. A Hot Mom is defined by her soul, her core. A Hot Mom is about being the best YOU, about being a woman who radiates confidence from the inside out. A Hot Mom is a woman who loves her family and herself but doesn't get lost in the madness of motherhood. A Hot Mom is empowered. A Hot Mom is a woman who knows how to balance *her* needs as well as the needs of her family. A Hot Mom is a BETTER mom! A Hot Mom is a BETTER lover! A Hot Mom is a BETTER friend! *Every* mom can be Hot Mom!

CHAPTER 1

"We cannot abandon who we were before we had children. Our personal goals and dreams also need to be nurtured."

—Nita Whitaker, Singer

B.C.
(BEFORE CHILD)

Motherhood gives us depth, compassion, and a level of love and awareness so heartfelt it is indescribable. When our children are born, so is this other person known as "Mom"—this ever-caring, protective, beck-and-call being. As mothers, we now have these souls we are responsible for. They come to us, or they come through us. We help mold them, teach them, and yet they are their own person, with their own destiny and connection to the world. It's important as moms, while we help shape and nurture our children's world, that we also keep nurturing and creating our own spirit.

All too often we try so hard to fit the mold of "good parent" or "perfect mom," it becomes easy to lose our self in the process. Believe me, I know. Like most moms, it wasn't long before my main focus and point of exis-tence seemed to be my son's comfort and happiness. My day revolved around errands and his activities. I com-pletely lost myself in this routine. Where was that confi-

dent, fun loving person I was B.C. (Before Child)? Did being a good mom mean that my spirit had to suffer? I kept thinking, this isn't supposed to be *my* life!

I was your classic over-achiever from a good family and nice small town. My life was textbook until about age twenty-four. I got pregnant with a man I hadn't been dating very long. We got married and we got divorced and there I was, to my shock and horror, twenty-six and a single mom. How could this happen to me? I was a "good girl." Where was my house, my husband, the dog and the 2.5 kids? I somehow believed that not having that "life" was the reason I was stuck in the Groundhog Day rut. It took me a long time to figure out that it wasn't my situation, but my perception of it and the distorted perception of motherhood. It sounds cliché but I realized if I wanted people to perceive me differently I had to change the way I perceived myself and my life. The moment my attitude changed is the moment everything changed.

> "As a child, I remember seeing glamorous pictures of my mom and other moms before they became mothers and I thought, what happened? Somehow, I felt guilty about it and wished my mom could go back to being a movie star. So when I had my babies, I made a firm decision that I would stay me. "
>
> —**Catherine Wayland, Editor and founder of *International Family Magazine***

The truth is, you can't be the best mom when you are holding back your true self, when you are filled with self-doubt or frustration. It is crucial to foster your spirit and your sexuality. You have to stay true to yourself and indulge GUILT FREE in the little things that make you happy. This no doubt makes you a more effective mother. The very first step to becoming a Hot Mom is to grab back your identity and discover or rediscover who you are!

> "You're not just the 'mother of some child.' You're not just 'someone's wife/girlfriend.' You're not just 'some company's female executive.' You're that wild child from high school, that cocky rebel from your early twenties. Remember her? She's there, just waiting to come out. You can still nurture and take care of your beautiful babies. Just don't lose your inner outlaw. Don't lose the fiery, sultry woman inside of you who lives life to its fullest with kids in tow, eyes aflame, and hair blowing in the wind."
>
> —Sheila Kelly, Creator of the SFactor

YOU DON'T LOOK LIKE "A MOM!"

People would often tell me, "Wow! You don't look like a mom!" I used to think, why not? What does a "mom" look like? We are so conditioned by a preconceived image of what a mom should be. For years, we've been trained to feel it's wrong if we want to stay hot as a

mom. We've been taught to believe that it somehow works against our abilities as a mother. This couldn't be further from the truth! It's completely normal to want to maintain elements of your former self: your sexiness, your desirability, YOU. It's so engrained within us that we have accepted and even promoted the idea that once a woman becomes a mom, she shouldn't be sexy or stylish anymore. I can't think of anything more ridiculous! But unfortunately, it's easy to fall into this trap because society leads us into this belief with such ease: A good mother has no time to care for herself, and you're a mother now...

> "You are your child's inspiration, and in knowing that, be the very best person that you can be."
>
> —**Karma McCain,**
> **Co-founder of**
> **the Hot Mom's Club**

Keeping the former parts of you alive actually *enhances* your abilities as a mother, lover, and friend.

"I believe Hot Moms need to adore ourselves just as we adore our children. We give so much of ourselves and expect so little in return. How about our needs as a person? Why do we just settle for being last on the list and count down the hours until that magic hour, after they're gone to sleep? Just because you think that's what's ex-

---

pected of you as a super mom? The only person who puts these high expectations on us is ourselves. We're our own worst enemy. If we don't look after ourselves mentally, physically, and emotionally, there's a huge hole in our soul and an extreme lack of self-worth. How is that going to help our children?"

—Tracey Mallett, Fitness expert

"We make our children the center of our lives, but I believe that the more of yourself you retain, the more you will feel happy, proud, and full of energy and the more you will have to give to your child."

—Tricia Leigh Fisher, Owner and founder of Nana's Garden

"Doing for others all the time doesn't mean you've done your job. I'm talking about giving our daughters (and sons) slightly better tools, with a strong united message that we can be even better mothers, wives, daughters, lovers, sisters, and workers when we remember to take time to nourish ourselves in deeply soul inspired ways. What's inside will shine out. That means spending time experimenting with something that's creatively passionate. Whether its music, poetry, painting, or dance, do something that makes your body move and your mind engage and your heart leap with the satisfaction that you have participated in bringing forth something utterly lovely from your soul. This is ultimately the core of an inspired life.

When we agree to bring a child into this world, we facilitate not only the repopulation of our species on some primal level, but we also agree to facilitate another human being's fruition of their potential. To do that, we must be actualizing our own potential—not merely through a duty-bound existence matched to our responsibilities but through each of our unique forms of self-expression."

—Joy Rose, Founder of MAMAPALOOZA

BE YOU.

It's time to be more than a mom. It's time to be every bit of everything that you are. It's time to be who you want to be and not who anyone else thinks you should be. It's time to be bold, to be smart, to be true to your inner self. It's time to embrace and nurture who you are because there is absolutely no one in the whole world like you—own that. Be you and be proud. Love that you bake cookies for school parties or love that you buy them. Love that you can dress a screaming three-year-old, make breakfast and pack four lunches in less than twenty minutes. Don't make light of any accomplishment! It's time for you to love who you are as a person and as a parent. As moms it's in our nature to constantly put everyone and everything else first. We rarely stop to do anything for ourselves. It's time to embrace YOU. You have the right to choose what type of woman you want to be after you have children.

"I find it critical for women to take care of themselves first: spiritually, emotionally, physically. If they do this, they will be well positioned to succeed as a mother, wife and a professional."

—Chynna Phillips, Singer and songwriter

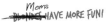
> "I am thirty-nine years old and a single mom of two boys, ages eight and twelve. Three years ago I took up freestyle BMX biking ramps, jumps, peg stalls and more—and I love it! Learning new skills on a bike over time has presented me a learning curve that I just can't rush. Through patience, dedication and new risks, I've found the courage in myself to face some fears and discover new strengths. My boys don't just see my riding as something their mom does; it is part of who their mom is. Their friends are always amazed that a mom could do something like this (so are their parents). I just know that age and gender are not issues for me when pursuing what moves my spirit. So be good to your heart. Live your passion."
>
> —Rochelle L'Italien, BMX mom

CULTIVATE YOUR SPIRIT AND CREATIVITY.

My son is the biggest, most amazing part of my life... but he is not my *entire* life. I say that in the healthiest, most loving way possible. It is so easy to get swallowed up in your kid's world. *Cultivating your spirit and creativity is just as important as cultivating theirs.* The best example you can set for your children is to have a life outside of them. This will give them the confidence to have a life outside of you. So, when you're with your kids, be *with* them. But when you are not, be you! Talk about the things that *you* are doing and make sure you are doing enough things worth talking about. You can drop your kids at dance class, but don't forget to go dancing now and then with your girlfriends.

> "Getting a life means getting a life outside your life, a life that really comes from the deepest place inside you! It's not about adding to your already overflowing schedule. It does take a certain amount of time and commitment to find your creative expression, but it's AMAZING how much more energy you will have when you find something you love to do, for no other reason than you love to do it. My only advice is if you want to be a Hot Mom for the next fifty years, make sure to take the time to figure out who you are when you take your apron off at night."
>
> —Joy Rose, Founder of MAMAPALOOZA

"I am a mother of two boys, Zico (nine) and Tosh (six). Before I became a mom I was very active and very carefree. I was rarely stressed or worried about life. But after I became a mom things changed, namely me. I forgot who Chani was. I was totally consumed with being a super mom. Even my husband moved down on my list of priorities. Then I started Moms On Boards which is a business/club that supports and connects moms like me who love to surf, snowboard, skateboard, wakeboard, etc. My mission is to honor, celebrate, recognize, represent, and encourage moms from all walks of life to live proudly and find the one thing that nurtures their spirit and feeds their soul."

—Chani Demello, a.k.a. "M.O.B. boss" and
Founder of Moms On Boards

CREATE HARMONY.

Remember life is about balance, and creating harmony is crucial for the well-being of your children. Our kids can be our greatest inspiration for creating harmony. *When you weave your spirit into motherhood, the possibilities are endless.*

"There's nothing more amazing than a mom fulfilling her dreams and pursuing a career on her own terms. From the moment we discover we are going to be mothers, we prepare ourselves to sacrifice everything for the well-being of our families.

When I started Wyatt-MacKenzie Publishing Inc., Wyatt was fifteen-months-old and MacKenzie was six-weeks. At that time they did not appreciate the books on the shelves with their names on it. Now they are seven and eight and they are filled with pride when one of my 'mom authors' is on TV, and that *their* books can be found in the library!

You must find what brings you joy and surround yourself with it. Find others who share your passion and observe what they have done. Moms holding on to their dreams are a powerful example for their children to realize their own dreams and to not settle for anything less than doing what they love."

—Nancy Cleary, Publisher

"From the second my son Troy was born, everything took on a different shade. Many things became gray, falling quickly into the background, and some things became more obvious and crystal clear. Some things that used to seem so important to me now felt silly. To realize I had this little being in my arms, that I was responsible for guiding his life was so awe-inspiring that words can't even describe the feeling. The next year I was completely devoted to the commitment of mirroring the best of him and imprinting the best of my husband and myself. I chose not to work, except a bit here and there, besides I was only feeling inspired to be a mother to my son. I really didn't feel I had any other type of creativity flowing through me. That was pretty scary after being a musician and singer-songwriter my whole life. There were times I thought 'Okay, now what? I was a musician for twenty-years and now I am a mother. This is who I am now! Will I ever be a musician again? Will I ever even want to be?' Then I started recharging my creativity in ways I had never experienced. From day one, beautiful melodies would pop in my head that I would just start singing to Troy. Funny songs too, about what I imagined he was thinking. Cool beats and fun lyrics all in my head, coming from my heart. I started to keep a small recorder next to the rocking chair...and there I was still rocking...just in a different way!

Now looking back sixteen months and a new CD later, I realize I was doing what I had always done but in such a profoundly different way I almost didn't trust it. It was so effortless and so inspired. I wasn't used to the writing and recording process of a CD (which had never been an easy or particularly fun process) coming to me so easily. This has been the best writing and recording experience of my entire life and many have told me it is their favorite record of mine. Being a mom unleashed a new found artistic freedom unlike any other. Because I was so connected and present with my baby, I organically tapped into another side of my creativity by entering into that innocent world of exploration and wonder. Funny how my newest incarnation of trying to be the best mom I could be and being so happy with that job, produced the most inspired music of my entire career."

—Meredith Brooks, Grammy-nominated artist

Motherhood broadens us and adds strength to our character. It gives us an entirely new perspective on life. Our children open and expand our world in so many ways. In order to provide them the best possible life, you

must be the best possible YOU. And you owe it to your children to create the brightest light within yourself so you can have more to give them. Only you know what best raises and stirs your spirit. The first step to becoming a Hot Mom is to find your core. *Let motherhood enhance you.* It is then and only then that your mothering can take flight.

> "Think of your heart like the sun, shining upon these new little beings. Too much sun can burn their leaves, too little, and they can wilt. Shine your loving gorgeous heart-light upon them and watch what happens."
>
> —Diana Lang, Author of *Opening to Meditation*

REFLECTIONS

- Are you happy with who you are now?

- What do you do to cultivate your spirit and creativity?

- Is there balance in your life?

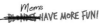

COMMITMENTS

- Commit to discovering or rediscovering YOU.

- Commit to following your dreams and passions so you can be the best mom you can be.

- Commit to creating balance and harmony between your needs and your child's.

CHAPTER 2

"The most perfect thing about us

is that we are imperfect."

—**Goldie Hawn, Actress**

CHAPTER 2

I AM ONE HOT MOM!

I know, I know. Your body isn't the same after having one kid or five kids. Of course not! *Your body has performed one of the most awe-inspiring human feats.* With supermodels in every magazine and on every billboard, it's tough to maintain a healthy self-image, even before your body has been stretched and reshaped and kicked from the inside. It has taken me a long time, but I've realized it's more important

> "…a person's worth is defined by who you are, who you bring into the world, and how you treat people, your contributions to your personal relationships and the bigger picture…that is what makes you a Hot Mom."
>
> **—Jeanine Lobell, Founder of Stila cosmetics**

how you perceive yourself than how others perceive you. Unfortunately, most women have a false self-image.

Living in Los Angeles, I have met some of the most beautiful women in the world, and guess what? They have asked me if their butt looks too fat in their jeans, complained that their arms are too long, nose is too big, or ears too stuck out. I've heard it all and thought, "Are

you kidding me? You are walking perfection! How on earth can you feel this way?"

So you're probably wondering, what does this have to do with me as a mother? EVERYTHING. Your children learn their relationship with their bodies, their self-image—they learn it all from you. So if you don't like who you are, how can you expect them to like who they are?

JUST THE WAY YOU ARE.

My son has two crazy cowlicks and no matter what gel or mousse I use, by the end of the day his hair goes in a hundred different directions. I find it adorable. I purposely keep his hair long because I love it so much. It's unique to him and it always makes me smile. My hair also has a mind of its own, however I don't always find it so cute when it won't cooperate.

> "A Hot Mom knows if you can't find happiness within, you won't find it without."
>
> — **Rasheda Ali, Daughter of Mohammed Ali**

One day, my son saw me struggling to flatten a piece of my hair. He came up next to me and started flattening his own hair. He kept getting more and more frustrated when it wouldn't hold in place. I told him I loved his hair "just the way it is." After I said this, he turned to me and said, "Mom, I love your hair *just the way it is.*" Wow. His words hit me hard.

We owe it to our children to fall in love with ourselves, just as we are. Commit to loving what you were given and loving what you've done with it. It's time to love the shape of your hips, the gap between your teeth, the fact that no one in the whole wide world looks like you and never will. Love your

"If you pour energy into what you don't have you'll have nothing. Pour it into what you do have and the world will lay itself at your feet."

—Joy Rose, Founder of MAMAPALOOZA

uniqueness, your imperfections. Love being thirty-one, forty-five, fifty-seven or eighty. Love the age you are and the wisdom you have gained. Know, and I mean really know, how beautiful and unique you are.

FALL IN LOVE WITH YOURSELF.

Your primary relationship is with yourself and all of your other relationships reflect this. The more you learn to love and appreciate who you are, the more love and appreciation you will receive. How you feel about yourself determines the quality of your life, your relationships, your healing, and your capacity to succeed. The bond you form with yourself is one of the biggest spiritual challenges you'll face. As much and as deeply as you love your children, it is equally important to fall madly, unabashedly in love with yourself! Love yourself

with every ounce of your being and you will teach your children to love themselves the same way.

ALWAYS FIND THE FANTASTIC.

Take a few minutes and think about what makes you fantastic. It may be difficult at first because we often feel awkward stating anything positive about ourselves. But the more you apply the principals and exercises in this handbook, the more your confidence will build and the easier it will be to acknowledge the things you love about yourself. Try keeping a list in your purse or by your bed of all the things that you love about you. Write what you can for now but if you add one thing each week you will find something so freeing about acknowledging your in-

> "We all want to be brilliant, talented and beautiful. If you look in your children's eyes, you will see that you are!"
>
> —**Alicia Brandt, Co-founder of Women's Night Out**

credible self! It's also good to acknowledge and write down the fantastic things about the people closest to you. *The more you focus on the beauty of other people, the more you will start to discover your own beauty and strengths.* Find the fantastic in your friends, family, and children, and be sure to share with them what you find.

IT'S ALL ATTITUDE.

For those of you who are reading this and thinking, "I'm not hot"...think again. *Being a Hot Mom has nothing to do with age, race, size, or situation.* It has everything to do with attitude. You just have to believe it. It's all in your confidence and perception of yourself. It starts in your mind. It's how you CHOOSE to view yourself. Perception manifests reality.

"It's important to be a Hot Mom. Being in a positive space is so crucial for establishing your children's self-confidence."

—**Daniella Clarke, Designer**

"If I could wave a magic wand, confidence is the gift I would give every woman in this world. It is the first thing that every woman needs in order to be sexy, especially moms. Confidence is what makes a mom hot. Confidence makes a woman rock. It's what makes her sexy and makes her man want her like nothing else! With so many people to care for and so much to juggle, it is a mom's confidence that will see her through when all else fails. Please don't look for anyone else to give confidence to you. If your sense of self comes from another person, they can take it away from you as quickly as they gave it. You

> must develop a rock solid sense of yourself. A woman can't feel good about herself if she's always focusing on what's wrong with her. If all you see is every little dimple on your thigh or extra inch on your waist, it will be difficult to have confidence. So you've got to start by being your own best friend."
>
> —Eve Michaels, Image consultant

Repeat the Hot Mom mantra, "I am one Hot Mom!"
There is enormous power in affirmations and mantras.

Affirmation:
Something asserted as being true. A positive statement proclaiming the goal the speaker or thinker wishes to achieve is already happening.

Mantra:
An expression or idea that is repeated. A sacred word or chant to facilitate spiritual power.

You become what you believe and what you believe affects how you feel and how you treat yourself, your children, your husband, your friends, etc. Put this book down and shout "I AM ONE HOT MOM!" Go on. Say it with attitude. "I AM ONE HOT MOM! I AM ONE HOT MOM! I AM ONE HOT MOM!" Yell at the top of your lungs, "I AM ONE HOT MOM!" Sing it. Inform all of your friends and family (and maybe even a few strangers) that they are in the presence of a Hot Mom. Say it every day, every hour, for as long as it takes until you truly believe it. Insist your friends introduce you as Billy's Hot Mom. Write Hot Mom in lipstick on your mirror. Have business cards made that say Jennifer, Hot Mom of (list your kids). If this seems silly, good! Hot Moms are silly. We're allowed to have fun. Hot Moms don't take the world or themselves too seriously.

"How do I stay Hot with two grown kids, a fifty-year-old body and a twenty-six-year marriage? A positive outlook and attitude. Your positive attitude becomes contagious, which affects your environment and everyone around you. That is how I stay HOT!"

—Andrea Frank Henkart, Author

Call it your mantra. Call it your affirmation. Call it whatever you want, just start today and start calling yourself a Hot Mom. You can use this positive self-talk in all areas of your life. It's unbelievably effective. Try it and you'll see. If your mind starts chattering back at you, with

"A Hot Mom is a mother that has confidence and raises her children with values and tons of love. *A confident mother is a confident child.*"

—Carnie Wilson, Singer and songwriter

thoughts like "No, that's not going to happen" or "Nah, not me," squash those negative messages immediately. Replace them with only positive reassurance. After all, YOU ARE ONE HOT MOM!

REFLECTIONS

- Do you LOVE who you are?

  _____

  _____

  _____

- What are your assets? What are the most fantastic things about you?

  _____

  _____

  _____

- What can you start telling yourself today to remind yourself that you are a Hot Mom?

  _____

  _____

  _____

COMMITMENTS

- Commit to loving yourself just as you are.

- Commit to finding all that is fantastic about you, your friends, and family. Search for the fantastic in everyone.

- Commit to telling yourself daily that "I AM ONE HOT MOM!"

CHAPTER 3

"If your computer softwear is

more current than your clothing...

it's time to change!"

—Eve Michaels, Image Consultant

DITCH THE SWEATS!

It's so easy to fall into the comfort rut. It's what I refer to as your "sweats." Sweats represent choosing convenience but as a result you sacrifice yourself. It's time to *ditch the sweats,* and I mean that as figuratively as I do literally. A Hot Mom takes charge of her looks and charge of her life and this chapter is all about leaving your comfort zone behind. It's time to clean out your closet and clean out your life. The two work in tandem.

Your outside should reflect your inside. And as you take better care of your spirit, you will naturally want to take better care of yourself in all areas. Let go of how a "mom" should dress and dress in the way that best reflects you! Your appearance, makeup, hair, and clothes are as important as your smile. Projecting an image of confidence sets you up for success.

The hardest part is deciding you are worthy of keeping yourself up and allowing time in your day to do it. As moms, we rarely even put ourselves on our to-do list. Although the truth is, it really doesn't take as much time

to maintain ourselves as we think. The hardest part is mentally getting past the idea that this somehow makes us vain. A healthy attitude starts on the inside, knowing and owning it. The next step is showing it.

A positive self-image is a crucial part of our emotional well-being. The best way to teach confidence and a healthy attitude to your children is to first have one yourself, then reflect it in the way you look, walk, and talk. *Give your appearance the attention it deserves, because you deserve it.*

As moms we are multitasking goddesses, so taking a few minutes in the morning to get yourself together is not out of the question if you make it a priority. Do whatever it is that makes you feel instantly beautiful. Brush on some lip gloss, tie on a bright colored scarf, or get that haircut you've been putting off. For those of you who think this makes you too self-important, I say get over that fast! I don't know a single person who doesn't leave the salon without that "I can take over the world" attitude. It sounds silly but it's true! Look at your children. See how they strut after a hair cut? Or when they have a new outfit? New shoes? It's natural as long as it comes from the right place. So start today and make improvements you can visually see. It's truly amazing what little changes can do for your psyche and self-esteem.

YOUR PERSONAL STYLE.

As you become more comfortable with your body and your inner essence, you will want to express that through your personal style. Clothes are a great tool for expressing your personality. Let's face it—it's hard to feel hot when you are covered in head-to-toe sweats. Now, I'm not suggesting you prance around all day in heels and a gown, but let your outside reflect your inside. Wear clothes that show off who you are. Take pride in your appearance.

> "Several months after my son was born I was having a conversation with some co-workers. An older fellow joked, 'Hey, is that the new style these days?' He was pointing to my husband's white gym socks peeking out below my black slacks. He continued to joke saying 'You used to be so hip...what happened?' That moment was a huge wake up call for me. I realized that it only takes another minute in the morning to accessorize myself with matching items like jewelry, shoes, and *my own socks*! I feel put together and my day seems to run smoother because I take that extra moment to be a chic, Hot Mom."
>
> —Kailynn Bowling, Co-founder of ChicBlvd

CLEAN OUT YOUR CLOSET!

Right now, go straight to your closet and take out every thing you haven't worn in a year. It's time to clean out! Dedicate some time to combing through all the stuff that has built up over the months or years or *decades*. Don't be afraid, it's actually liberating. So go ahead and get rid of that blazer with the big shoulder pads or those jeans that rest above your naval. I'm quite sure they aren't coming back in style.

It's okay to keep things with sentimental value, but don't be scared to let go. Getting rid of the old makes room for the new. Be brave! You're a Hot Mom and it's time to recreate yourself. *Style is all about knowing who you are, being proud of that person and expressing her in any way you feel comfortable.* It's okay to treat yourself to some new things—you deserve it! So quit feeling guilty. Just because you are a mom doesn't mean you can't keep yourself up or create a new sense of style. Hot Moms try new colors and cuts, new jeans and new dresses. Don't ever let "I'm a mom" or "I'm too old for that" stop you from buying something you really like. Your wardrobe should reflect your attitude, your confidence, your sense of fun and adventure.

If the thought of paring down your prized possessions is a little too overwhelming for you, host a "Clean Out Your Closet" party. I throw one every season. I give all of my friends two-weeks notice to go through their closets and drawers. Then, we all get together at my place with our bags of clothes and exchange. It's a blast! We have a little wine, some chocolate and a lot of laughs. Everyone ends up going home with something "new" to add to her wardrobe. Whatever is left over is donated to a women's shelter. This turns a tedious task into something fun to look forward to.

"The Haute Mom's Arsenal" by Carilyn Vaile, Designer

As the mother of two little budding fashion plates, I take my role as a Hot Mom very seriously. In addition to wanting to look good for myself and my husband, I want to set an example for my girls that fun and fashion don't have to end once you've started a family. Looking good is important for girls of all ages, but somehow it seemed much easier to pull it all together when there wasn't a little one pulling on your best sweater and turning your favorite tank top into the perfect gown to wear while trying out their new paint set.

I hear it all the time from my friends who are moms: there's no time to shop anymore, and if there is, you somehow find yourself gravitating more to-

wards grabbing that comfy 6X instead of your sexy size 6. And then of course, some of those former size 6's just don't fit the way they used to. Isn't it easier to stick to a uniform of ratty jeans and a comfy sweater if your kid is just going to squirt their juice box on it anyway?

My answer is a resounding NO! C'mon, you didn't start eating food from a jar just because your baby did, did you? So why would you settle for looking drab and boring when there are so many better options? I'm not asking you to invest tons of time and money— just set aside a little of each to develop your secret weapon: The Haute Mom's Arsenal.

FABULOUS FOUNDATION

Underneath every Haute Mom you will find some sexy underwear. Don't worry, I'm not saying you need to give up all your comfy cotton bras and undies, but every mom occasionally faces a situation where she wants to feel like more than a mom, and the best place to begin is with what you *can't* see.

JEANS TO SUIT YOUR GENES

No matter where you live or what you do, a pair of good jeans is essential to every Haute Mom's wardrobe. In recent years, denim has become dressier, and you simply must have at least one pair that you can slip on (or, these days, squeeze into, holding your breath as you use a pair of pliers to pull up the zipper) to feel young, cool, and sexy. You also need jeans to wear around the house, but these too should fit you in a flattering way. There's nothing wrong with boyfriend jeans, as long as you don't actually look like him in them. You're a woman and you should be proud of it, so add a funky belt to show off that waist—or to hide a slight tummy bulge—and you're good to go.

ACCESSORIES: THE ICING ON YOUR CAKE

It is the little accents to your wardrobe that offer up Haute Mom status: newsboy hats, individualized fashion jewelry, gorgeous scarves tied with a special flair. These little additions go beyond the basics and are essential to a Haute Mom's wardrobe because they can make "basic" look anything but.

It is through accessories that your look becomes unique. Maybe you're someone who loves mixing leather and lace. Maybe you love using baroque pins to fasten your blazer—whatever seems like fun to you will brighten up any outfit. Acquiring a variety of pieces may take some time, but that is the fun part. It's a great excuse to play dress up just like we did when we were kids!

Take a note from my four-year-old daughter. I love watching her play dress up. She puts her outfits to-

gether with such care and she has no inhibitions. I guarantee you will never hear a young girl turn down a feather boa with the excuse: "That's not really me." She knows it can be "her" one moment, and something else will be "her" the next. She inspires me so much, but I also know that the way I dress influences her enormously. Our children learn from our examples. When your daughter sees you not taking the time to bring out your best self, what does that tell her about motherhood? We must set the example of how to be Haute Moms so it becomes innate in our daughters. They deserve it and we are worth it, so don't skimp on the accessories.

A CLIFF-NOTES CLOSET

This is the final tip, but it may be the most important one for those of you who really feel overwhelmed by putting together a presentable look. For those five minute mornings when you are tempted to default to the sweats and tees, I suggest the Haute Mom have a go-to area or "Cliff Notes" version of your closet. This is where you keep the outfits and items you can turn to in an emergency to achieve Haute Mom status. These pieces should be tried and true, easily accessible, and ready at a moment's notice. Dresses are perfect to keep in this area since they take no time to put on—allowing you more time to play with your accessories and shoes! Plus, dresses are so versatile. I have one in my current collection called "The Ten Ways Dress," because you can put it on ten different ways to achieve ten different styles.

The Haute Mom is a prepared mom, so always make sure to launder or dry clean your "go-to" articles of clothing routinely. You never know how quickly you may need to wear them again, and you don't want to be stuck without them!

I hear my daughter's voice beckoning; luckily I've shared all the tips I have! Remember, these are the basics. As a Haute Mom, you will likely be able to combine them with your own tried and true fashion rules, but if you follow these tips, I guarantee in no time you'll be feeling haute, haute, haute.

CLEAN OUT YOUR LIFE!

Just as you assessed your closet, now it's time to take a look at your life. How many times a day do we tell our kids to clean up their messes? Stop and take a look at what's messy in your life. It may be a relationship with your sister, mother, in-law, co-worker, friend, husband, or ex. You fill in the blank: whoever, whatever. Do what you need to do to heal and get over it, to move on and let it go. Often we hold on to things because we are afraid we don't deserve more. I urge you to trust and let go. Release anything weighing you down or holding you back. Make an effort to speak to a professional who can help you work through your emotions and really commit to solving the problem. It is impossible to be free and confident if you have negative energy surrounding you. A Hot Mom doesn't have time for drama, so clean out your life!

As with your closet, keep only the relationships that make you feel good. It is so important to surround yourself with friends who are positive and fun. You become who you hang out with. Make room in your life for wise souls and people who inspire you. Just as you wouldn't encourage your kids to hang around with anyone that isn't good for them, make sure those closest to you have traits and characteristics that motivate and propel you forward. Decide what or who needs to go in your life and make room for more of what you want. And as with those new clothes you'll purchase, don't be afraid to befriend someone colorful and new.

LET GO.

Let go of the way you thought your life was supposed to be and enjoy what it has become. For a long time I attached myself pretty concretely to "the dream." Believe me, my plan did not include being a single mom. I struggled with this for a long time. I felt guilty over what I did wrong. I felt angry about what my ex did wrong. I was mad at the world and mad at myself. I wasted a lot of time blaming my ex and myself for my situation. But I quickly learned that negative attitudes and energy only create more negative attitudes and energy. Break the cycle. I did.

Whatever you are holding on to in your life, LET IT GO. Letting go of judgment and negativity has no downside. *You owe it to your children to forgive.* Start by forgiving yourself—no one is perfect. We are all growing and learning every day. There is enormous healing and power in forgiveness.

> "It is important to deal with negative feelings and energy because it affects how you relate to yourself and others. What you are feeling on the inside is always a match for what you attract on the outside. To be a Hot Mom let go of your negative energy and monitor your thoughts so they are positive. Every thought creates a feeling. Are you having the kind of thoughts that are giving you a sparkle, enthusiasm, and which make other people want to be in your company?"
>
> —Dr. Evelyn Budd Michaels, Counselor

Let go of all your regrets. You are choosing and creating your life every day. So release the need inside to make everything perfect. Release your inner, wounded child's authority over you. If they aren't healed, wounds keep us living in the past. Dwelling on them will not do anything to help you right now, so no matter how hard your past tugs at you, focus on where you are and where you want to be in the future. Make choices that will get you there. The bottom line is you are in control of your life. *Teach your kids they can take charge of their lives by taking charge of yours.*

I have made many mistakes. I make new ones every day, but I've quit concentrating on them and I've started learning from them. One of the biggest mistakes I made was being afraid to take a chance, staying in a situation when my spirit knew it was time to leave. I have learned if you let your soul guide you and you bring your confidence along for the journey, you'll always land on your feet. The hardest part is deciding to do it, to ditch the "sweats." So while you are cleaning out your life, don't forget to toss away all of your insecurities and fears.

A Hot Mom is bold. A Hot Mom knows who she is. A Hot Mom keeps what she wants and needs in life and lets go of anything she doesn't.

REFLECTIONS

- What is your personal style?

- What clutter is weighing you down or holding you back?

- Are you holding on to negativity? Are you surrounding yourself with encouraging, wonderful people? If not, why?

COMMITMENTS

- Commit to letting your clothes reflect your personality and confidence.

- Commit to wearing an outrageous pair of panties to your next PTA meeting, just for fun!

- Commit to tossing out those old clothes, old grudges, old insecurities, and old fears.

CHAPTER 4

"When I was pregnant, my doctor told me to exercise a little less than I normally would… uh, *that would be a coma.*"

—**Stephanie Blum, Comedienne**

BODY AFTER BABY

As a mom, it's more important than ever to take care of your body. Honoring your body is just as important as honoring your mind and spirit. Our body and soul are intended to work together. So treat your body as your temple. Eat right and exercise! Hot Moms take care of themselves. NO EXCUSES. Why? It affects your mood, your energy, your physical and mental health.

COMMIT.

Fitness is a lifelong commitment. Initially as moms, we might be motivated to get back our pre-prego bods. And while this is important, it misses the essence of why you should change your life through exercise. Regular exercise will alter you in ways you would never have thought. Making a commitment and sticking to it is a huge accomplishment. The act of

"I know getting back in shape is a hard commitment and almost feels unattainable, but you really can do it. You're the Hot Mom in control. You only have one body and if you look after your body as if it were your shrine, it will look after you, keeping you young, energetic and full of life."

—Tracey Mallett, Fitness expert

getting up and walking several times a week—actually doing it and keeping your promise—will enhance your self-esteem dramatically. You'll feel good about yourself and you'll feel empowered. There is a significant mental component to fitness. *If you let it, exercise can be a vehicle to tremendous spiritual growth.* Try setting up a program and setting some goals to experience levels of achievement. A good exercise program builds your spirit as well as your muscles.

"After having my second of three sons, I decided to find a way to get back into shape, to feel good about myself after months of sleepless nights and baby-vomit-stained over-sized t-shirt wearing. I decided to do something I've always dreamed of doing, train for and run a marathon. I was motivated by the fact that I was becoming a lean, mean mommy machine. I ran with the double baby jogger or got up at five a.m. to catch the sunrise and greet the day. It was almost addicting; the run, the accomplishment, the hot shower afterward. I'll never forget during my second marathon, seeing my husband with my two sons sitting in my very worn, double baby jogger on the side of the road near the water stop cheering for me, 'Go Mommy! Go!' My heart just warmed up and raced with joy! I couldn't believe it. I had two small children, I was running a marathon, and they were watching me. My sons saw a role model of what a strong woman is and should be and I get to be the best mom ever because I am content with myself and what I have accomplished!"

—Beth Aldrich, Founder of the TV series
For Her Information

INCORPORATE THE KIDS.

Get creative and find a way to get those endorphins flowing every day. Walk with the kids, jump rope with the kids, swim, dance, go to the gym, run up and down your stairs ten times, or run after your three-year-old. Find out what interests you and DO IT! There is a release that fits into every schedule.

"How do I stay hot as a mom? Walking with my kids at water parks and zoos."
—**Kelly Preston, Actress**

Before I had my son, I worked out consistently every day. After his birth, it seemed I ran more errands than laps around the track. I had to find a way to incorporate my fitness routine into motherhood. You don't need fancy machines or expensive gym memberships. All you need is a

pair of sneakers and you are on your way. Walk with friends. Walk with the stroller. Join a group or go alone. Walk. Walk. Walk. It will clear your head and tone your muscles. Next time you are tempted to drive three blocks to the park (don't laugh, we've all done it!), grab your stroller and walk.

> "As mothers, it is our job to provide a healthy platform from which our children can learn and grow. When they watch us fit exercise into our busy lives, they inadvertently mimic our actions and become healthy, active adolescents, then adults.
>
> It doesn't take much to incorporate fitness into our lives after baby. A walk in the park breathing the fresh air benefits both mother and baby. Get reacquainted with your old favorite workout video during naptime. Join one of the numerous child-friendly fitness programs that use baby for strength training segments. Or take advantage of the daycare facility offered in most athletic clubs. Spend some quality time with family members strolling through your neighborhood after dinner, or find a group of stroller moms in your neighborhood who run or walk together."
>
> —Andrea Vincent, Founder of
> SeeMOMMYrun

Dance is one of the most social ways to get your aerobic training in. It instantly boosts your spirit and vitality. I have danced with my son since he was a baby. Some of my favorite memories are of him giggling uncontrollably as I danced with him in my arms doing little dips and funny motions. He's now six and still loves to dance around. So turn up your favorite song and GO FOR IT!

Bike with the kids, take a hike, or swim with them. There are so many ways to incorporate fitness into your routine. There are endless ways to stay active and healthy. Find something you love. Try something new and make it work for you. Just make it happen. Working out shouldn't be a chore. Make it fun. *There has got to be something that moves you.*

> "Set a good healthy example for your kids. My four-year-old daughter, Amber, loves doing pilates and yoga with me. I caught her showing her friends some ABB exercises. They were tickled pink trying to do a single leg stretch from Pilates and a downward dog in yoga. It was very funny to watch and most importantly, they associated exercise as a fun activity. This is excellent to install at a young age."
>
> **—Tracey Mallett, Fitness expert**

"Growing up, always battling my weight was not easy. Becoming a mother has given me a foundation and a sense of pride that allowed me to overcome all

85

my fears and trials. It was not until after I became pregnant that I got real with my health. I realized the importance of a new beginning, not only for this precious human being that was growing inside of me, but for myself. It was as if a higher power greater than myself enlightened me to the truth that I must take better care of myself in order to take better care of my child. So I started on my journey. Not the hurry-up-and-get-skinny-in-two-weeks method. Instead I employed the honest way of first starting to truly love myself. With me, after beginning to practice self respect and self love, my food plan and exercise routine fell right into place. I looked forward and actually craved my workouts. I treated my gym time as a business meeting I could not miss with the most important person in the world: myself. My body instinctually desired nutritious foods and balanced meals. I started to meditate and treat myself to the necessary downtime and rest required when being a mother. Understanding that I was about to start the most important chapter in my life, I knew that embracing a new healthy lifestyle was crucial. I am a happier, more energetic mother and I owe it all to taking care of myself! I am a living example of how one can make positive improvements in their life not only to better themselves, but also to bet-

> "Hot Moms need food for the body, food for the mind and food for the soul."
>
> —**Chris Georgas, Private chef**

ter the quality of life to those precious around them. I know about weight loss and what it takes to keep it off. I shed over seventy pounds after the birth of my second son. Being active has made me a better mother because I have a more positive outlook on parenting and life in general. I also have more energy. When people ask me what I do, I tell them I am an athlete. Normally the second question is: What sport? My answer is: I am a mom. They look at me funny for a second, but then it sinks in. You can see the thought processing in their head. Being a mom is full-time, with full-time physical demands that is a never-ending marathon!"

—Jennifer Nicole Lee, Ms. Muscle & Fitness (2006), Ms. Bikini America (2005)

WHAT'S FOOD GOT TO DO WITH IT?

The quality of your life begins at the nourishment level. What you put on the inside absolutely effects how you look and feel on the outside. As moms, we sometimes focus so much on making sure our kids are fed, we often forget to eat ourselves. And no, a stolen bite or two of a peanut butter and jelly sandwich doesn't constitute a healthy lunch, even if you have four kids! As moms we run it all, and we can't afford to get sick. Same as our

kids, when we are hungry we get irritable and moody, and wrong foods make us lethargic and grumpy. Hot Moms make their food work for them.

NOURISH YOUR BODY.

Know the difference between feeding your hunger and nourishing your body. Take some time and really focus on what you are putting into your body and why. Are you eating because you are bored or rushed? Because you are upset, or simply because it's lunchtime? As moms we are often so busy and don't want to spend a lot of energy or time on food, often grabbing whatever is easiest. Regardless, be aware of your eating habits. Work toward deliberate eating for strength and energy.

"Every healthy relationship has boundaries. Steady, stable, secure, life-affirming boundaries. The sort your mom set for you. Your only hope for lifelong health and fitness is to create a healthy relationship with food. By practicing portion control you can bring boundaries to your plate. Portioning your food allows you to have the ultimate safety net. My philosophy in life and with food is 'less is more.' Derive more pleasure from less and enjoy the benefits."

—Carrie Wiatt, Nutritionist, Author of *Eating by Design*

Break the habit of mindless or convenient nibbling.

Chemically laden and processed foods are a burden to the body. Even small amounts of toxins accumulate and wear it down. Be kind to your body. Keep your diet as pure as possible.

QUICK ENERGY BOOSTERS:

- The quickest and easiest way to boost your energy and complexion is to drink water. So often we eat when we are actually just thirsty. (You should drink at least 1/3 of your body weight in ounces of water a day). Many moms suffer chronic dehydration and are always tired. Headaches and lack of energy are both symptoms. Water flushes out the impurities, it helps enhance your mood; it's an absolute necessity. Start each day with a big glass of water. It gets your whole system going. Forget the soda and grab a glass of water now!

- Keep fruit in the house. It is the perfect snack for moms on the go. Fruit should be the main source of sweetness in your diet. Instead of robbing your body of essential nutrients like white sugar does, fresh fruit is filled with vitamin C. Besides, it's easy and cheap and requires no preparation time. I am also a huge fan of trail mix: nuts, berries, dried fruit, chocolate chips. Let your kids mix their own bags and always have it on hand.

- Choose green tea over coffee. It's a natural metabolism booster and antioxidant. Try honey as a sweetener.

- Eat six small meals a day rather than the traditional three square. You'll maintain a balance in your blood sugar level and the level of nutrients in your body.

We owe it to our children to model good eating and exercise habits. We owe it to ourselves, for our mood, strength, mental and physical health to find a diet and fitness program that fits our lifestyle and schedule. No excuses!

REFLECTIONS

- Do you have a fitness routine?

  _____

  _____

  _____

- What physical activities do you enjoy? How can you work them into your week?

  _____

  _____

  _____

- Be honest, how healthy do you eat? What can you add or subtract from your diet to increase energy and vitality?

  _____

  _____

  _____

COMMITMENTS

- Commit to setting goals and revel in your sense of accomplishment.

- Commit to an exercise routine and stick to it.

- Commit to developing healthy eating habits and drinking more water.

CHAPTER 5

"Replenish yourself so you have more to give to others."

—Andrea Frank Henkart, Author

CHAPTER 5

BREATHE

Hot Moms recognize that taking "time outs" to recharge, to get centered and balanced is crucial to being a good parent. There's no room to say you don't have time or your day is too hectic. As moms, we are multitasking goddesses. We juggle PTA meetings, the grocery store, soccer games, and all of this with a toddler strapped to our hips. We are nothing short of Hot Mom super heroes! If you choose to, you can find ten minutes in your day for your own "time out."

FINDING YOUR CENTER STARTS WITH YOUR BREATH.

Breath is the essence of life. Taking time to regulate your breath enhances your physical, emotional, and spiritual well-being. It is the key to health and happiness. Your breath integrates the many layers of your life.

Take a deep breath and hold it. Notice the discomfort that builds as you resist your natural impulses to exhale. When it's too uncomfortable, release your breath and

notice the immediate relief that sweeps over you. Holding on to anything when it is time to let go creates stress and discomfort in your body and mind.

Now completely empty your lungs and do not inhale. Pay attention to the discomfort that develops when you resist something you are meant to allow into your life. Breathing is a natural process of absorbing what we need and eliminating what we don't. *Each day take time to exhale some stress and invite in laughter and tranquility.* When you find yourself overwhelmed, take some of that age-old advice and "just breathe."

"A great exercise when you need a little sanctity is to make sure you are breathing deep enough so you can hear the inhales and exhales. Focus on that sound—this is the breath we use in yoga that helps us through some of the more challenging poses. It forces you to be present in the moment and stay calm. I use this technique with my girls when they become frustrated. We count to five or ten while following the sound of our breath. Try it. It will work calming wonders for you and for them."

—Elizabeth Blanchard, Yoga instructor

ENJOY THE PLEASURE OF YOUR OWN COMPANY.

Find time for you and you alone. Find silence now and then. What does that mean as a Hot Mom? We need time when it's totally quiet to think, to feel, to regenerate, and to access our inner self. Silent moments can be the most uncomfortable if we're used to all the noise around and inside of us. But honoring the need for total silence, alone or with others, can pave the way for being your authentic best. (Alone comes from the compound word ALL-ONE.)

MEDITATE.

You must indulge your mind daily with peace and quiet. The activity going on in your brain is communicated to every cell in your body. When your mind is cluttered every cell, tissue and organ is affected by that turbulence. You need to develop a method of calming and silencing your mind. This will generate a sense of peace and serenity throughout your entire body.

> "I get totally absorbed and focused on riding my bike when I'm in the midst of it; it's my moving meditation. I find it brings me inner peace."
>
> —**Rochelle L'Italien, BMX mom**

Meditation can help you temporarily escape a thought cycle and focus your attention. There are many ways to mediate so don't let it scare you. Meditation is actually quite simple. You can do it right now, right

where you are. The important thing is that you become still with yourself, that you become aware. Create an environment that lets your mind float free of thoughts. You can use music, soft chanting, or the sound of your own breath. Steal a few minutes while the kids are napping or when you're on your lunch break. Breathe deep and recharge. Find what works best for you, but in some way, everyday, focus on restoring your peace of mind.

> "Every time you meditate, you are building a spiritual muscle. The more you use it, the stronger it gets. The energetic apparatus you build by meditating will absolutely change the way your life works."
>
> —**Diana Lang, Author and Counselor**

> "Meditation helps you know where you are in time and space. When you understand where you actually are, it is easy to know what your next step is. All you have to do is open your heart to the light and energy that flows through you in every moment. That flow is always present. It is constant and perfect, always available to you. Meditation is constantly moving us inward and upward, lifting us to higher realms of understanding, creativity, and love."
>
> —Diana Lang, Author and Spiritual Counselor

Ignore whenever fatigue or frustration sets in and just breathe deep. Think of something calming. Find your touchstone. *It is lifesaving to know how to rejuvenate yourself.* You can meditate while walking, sitting, listening to music or snacking on a book. It's whatever brings you to a higher state of consciousness and helps you remain centered throughout the day.

For as long as I can remember, long, hot showers have been my salvation. Whenever I feel anxious or stressed I find sanctity under the steaming hot water. I didn't realize at first, but this was my meditation. It was my time to be free of distractions and pressures. It was my time to be completely engrossed with myself and my thoughts. I have since honed and polished my skills and have found additional paths to peacefulness that don't run up the water bill or leave my skin dry. My point is that you may already be meditating! Think about the things you do each day that force you to enter into yourself. Harness those things and make them work for you.

"Working out is the only time in my weekly schedule that's *my* time. It's my stress release, my religion and most importantly it keeps me sane. I get high on my endorphins and leave reality for thirty minutes. Heaven!"

—Tracey Mallett, Fitness expert

"I started dabbling in jewelry making when I was pregnant with my son Luca. The ideas just started flowing through me. Today designing continues to bring me such peace and comfort; it is a huge creative outlet and meditation."

—Janet Gunn, Jewelry designer

"I often find myself completely overwhelmed. Yes, even me, a yoga teacher. So many times I have chosen not to ask for someone's help and instead added a tenth task to my to-do list. But as minutes, hours, days, and months pass, I am wising up. I think we can all wise up by asking. Ask for a lending hand, even if it isn't from someone you know, but from a higher source. Sometimes it takes courage to ask—to ask for strength, grace, a blessing, an ounce of compassion, or a pinch of peace.

In moments when we feel overwhelmed, it is simple to sit down and meditate for three to five minutes. Here's how: If you can, retreat into a quiet room. Sit on the floor and cross your legs

Indian style or just sit in a chair. Bring your hands in front of you and cup them in front of your ribcage, your elbows at your sides. Your hands should be connected to each other as if you are making a big bowl with your hands. With your eyes closed, ask for simple grace. Allow your breath to be easy and smooth. Visualize every thing you're asking for coming to you in spades, overflowing into the bowl in front of you. Allow yourself to move forward in this grace for the rest of the day and you might find it easier to let go a little more than usual. Maybe it's okay to do one or two things at a time and not three, or four, or five, or six...I think you get my drift."

—Anna Getty, Creator of the
Divine Prenatal Yoga series

LOSE THE GUILT!

Like every mom, I used to feel so guilty if I wasn't with my son every minute of the day. The truth is we need time to ourselves, no matter how brief, to recharge and get centered. I can't repeat it enough, taking time for you every day, every week is essential. And the truth is, our kids need the space from us too.

A Hot Mom recognizes that doing things for *herself* makes her happy about doing things for others. If you feel like you never get to do anything you want to do, you will build resentment toward those around you for whom you are constantly doing things. Have absolutely no excuses and no guilt. I will say that again: NO GUILT! Take the time you need. You will be a better mother if you are refreshed and focused rather than worn too thin. Each week schedule a babysitter so you can have a little time to yourself. Work it into your budget—it's that important! Try a painting or a dance class. Catch a movie in the afternoon. Try yoga. Take a nap giving yourself completely to the regenerative power of sleep without reservation. Do whatever it is that you enjoy, mark it in your planner, and make it a priority. You deserve it. Don't wait for your husband or your mom to offer to watch the kids so you can go take a hike or get a massage. Schedule it and make it an appointment you can't miss. Take bubble baths or get pedicures. Do anything that makes you feel beautiful or alive. How you spend your time is up to you, but try to plan something just for you once a week.

> "To me, a Hot Mom doesn't take life too seriously or her kids too lightly."
>
> —**Kathie Lee Gifford, Mother of two**

"OXYGEN" by Carmen Richardson Rutlen, Author
(exerpt from *Dancing Naked...in fuzzy red slippers*)

When I used to sit on an airplane, waiting for take-off, I was always surprised and frankly horrified as the flight attendant presented her canned speech, while she pointed to the exits with arms moving in cheerleader-like precision, explaining how we could save ourselves if the plane were to fall from the sky.

What horrified me was not the thought of free falling from the sky, but rather the instructions given to mothers that in case of a drop in cabin pressure they were to put the oxygen masks on themselves first. Then and only then were they to put the masks on their children. It seemed so wrong, so cold, and so selfish—really bad.

Then I had a baby. The baby grew into a child. I discovered that extreme mothering could lead to oxygen deprivation for the mother. Devoting every moment of every day to fulfilling my child's slightest needs, wants, and whims became not only exhausting but also caused me oxygen starvation. I couldn't breathe.

One inspired day I came up for oxygen. I signed up for a watercolor class, two hours every Thursday night. One night a week of being unequivocally, self-lovingly, me. Not a mother, not an employee, not anybody's girlfriend, just me.

Ahh...the oxygen that came pouring through. That pure, clean, fresh oxygen allowed me to breathe, deeply. As I began to breathe deeper I noticed my son was breathing deeper too, as was my boyfriend, and it seemed, everyone around me.

I now take an oxygen break regularly, without guilt or a second thought, happy that in doing so I am showing my son and everyone who used to depend on me how to take in their own oxygen and breathe, deeply.

For all you working moms, when you're gone all day it's hard not to feel guilty about being away from your little ones. You may work because you have to or because you want to. Regardless, you are teaching your children that hard work is a necessary part of life and that working has no effect whatsoever on the amount of love you feel for them.

Keep in mind, you are doing the best you can. Guilt is an ineffective emotion and it doesn't change the facts. Make the best possible arrangements when you are working. Then when you are with your children, *be with them*. So often we come home and our mind is racing in a million different directions. Remember in these moments to slow down and breathe. Enjoy the sanctity of your home and the time with your kids. Leave the dishes in the sink. Run yourself a relaxing bubble bath after they've all gone to sleep. Sure, you may have to share it with a few rubber duckies and action figures, but a hot bath will most definitely help you clear your head and unwind. You've earned it, so enjoy and "just breathe." Guilt free!

REFLECTIONS

- Do you meditate? How do you find your center?

- What have you done recently for you? What would you like to do?

- Do you feel guilty about working or taking time out for yourself?

COMMITMENTS

- Commit to finding your touchstone, to finding something that brings you to a place of calm and peacefulness.

- Commit to carving out time for yourself each day to rejuvenate and recharge.

- Commit to losing the guilt associated with doing anything for yourself.

CHAPTER 6

— ❧ —

"There is nothing sexier or hotter
than being a mom."

—Cindy Margolis, Supermodel

EVERY MOM HAS AN INNER SIREN

Sexiness is a state of mind. It's wanting to feel desirable and in turn, allowing others to find you desirable. As moms, it's hard to feel sexy when you're changing stinky diapers all day, running on only a few hours of sleep, and showering so fast the mirror doesn't even fog. Just as these aspects of our life affect our sexuality, our sexuality affects every other part of our life. That is why it is so important to nurture *every* part of who you are, including your sexuality. It affects your happiness, your energy, and your confidence as a mother and woman. That's right, you are still a woman! It is sometimes easy to forget that and let the feminine, sexy side of you slide.

> "Our sexuality is a natural and healthy part of who we are as human beings."
> —Dr. Patti Britton, Clinical sexologist

Think you don't have an "inner siren?" Every woman has one. She may be buried behind those clothes you just

sniffed and pulled from the hamper, but I promise, she's in there and it's time to let her loose!

> "There exists in every woman an inner siren, a center of sexual power and self-knowledge. She's the wild, untamed part of you, your sexual alter ego, the opposite of the 'good girl.'
>
> By nature, women are sensual beings. Our breasts protrude, our butts stick out, our hips curve, and our waists indent. Many of us have been conditioned to hide or diminish our sexuality, our curves, our beauty. A Hot Mom is a woman who knows her inner siren. It's different for every woman. Maybe your inner siren is a playful 1940's pin-up or a Montana cowgirl or a pretty-in-pink baby doll or a leather-clad rocker chick or a bespectacled librarian or a French maid or an elegant Park Avenue seductress! Regardless of what your inner siren looks like, you have one. At times she may even be a combination of all of the above. Your inner siren has moods that evolve over time and defy simple labels. She's as idiosyncratic and beautiful as you are!"
>
> —Sheila Kelly, Creator of the Sfactor

The more comfortable you are with your sexuality, the sexier you will feel and the sexier you will be. It all starts in you. So let go of all those fears and insecurities and inhibitions. Who says moms can't be sexy? Who says that just because you are a mom that your femininity is no longer worth embracing? Being a mom only adds to your appeal. *As a mom, your depth for love and caring are stronger and greater than ever, so turn some of that love toward yourself.* Commit to dusting off your inner siren and letting her shine.

"It's important as a mom to stay in touch with the sexy side of you. If you neglect your sexy feelings then you also neglect your other feelings that can be shared with your loved ones. Feel, express, and share your vibrant, glowing, and loving energy. Be a Hot Mom and let your sexy side shine."

—Dr. Evelyn Budd Michaels, Counselor specializing in personal growth and development

Do something every day to nurture your inner siren, that sensual and beautiful woman inside of you. Take a trip to a lingerie store and buy some outrageous panties, then surprise your husband or wear them to your next PTA meeting just for fun. Test out sensual fragrant oils or

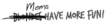

musks. Light a few candles and play a sexy CD. Take a steaming hot shower or eat a tantalizing meal. Ignite your taste buds and bring all your senses to life. Do whatever it is that makes you feel beautiful and helps you stay connected to the woman you are. Remember, sexiness is a state of mind and keeping the spark alive. Sexuality radiates not only from your physical body, but also from your subtle energy, your inner spirit. You are never too old and it's never too late to embrace your inner siren, so don't underestimate the sexual instincts you possess; the way you smile at someone, how you view your body, your receptivity to passion, or your ability to send it out. *Your inner siren is powerful.*

> "As long as there is life in you, you are never too old to try anything. There are so many men who are simply crazy about me. It's because of my attitude, my sexiness, my passion for life—it exudes from me."
>
> **—Moselle Amron, Championship dancer and eighty-one-year-old Hot Mom**

GET NAKED!

That's right, you heard me! Go to the mirror and take it all off. Take a good look. I know it can be scary and I know it may be hard, but really look at yourself and BE KIND. Our bodies have been criticized, judged and rejected by us for years. But starting today, you must focus on your assets and discover how beautiful and how exceptional you really are. Acknowledge your curves, the definition in your arms, or the color of your eyes. Acknowledge your hair or your cute little toes. The more willing you are to do this, to acknowledge your beauty as a woman, the easier it will become. Try saying this: "My body is more beautiful than ever!" By repeating this little mantra every day (each time you're in the shower or in front of the mirror), your body and mind will respond to this appreciation and you will grow increasingly more beautiful, inside and out. You will feel lighter. You will glow. *The effects of loving your body will truly astound you.*

KNOW THY BODY.

It doesn't matter whether you are married or single, knowing your body will add a healthy dimension to any relationship you're in. Remember the more you love, know and nurture yourself, the more you will want to love, know and nurture others.

> "Know where your hot spots are. Maybe you are turned on by a loving caress on your cheek or being teased with a feather on your ribs. Get to know your own body and what turns you on, whether it's the traditional kinds of places and moves or the unusual."
>
> —Dr. Patti Britton, Clinical sexologist

A good understanding of your body is essential to your emotional happiness and sexual health. I know it can be scary, giving your body the time and attention it deserves, but it's your body and you have every right to know it and nurture it. Having knowledge of your body will create in you enormous power and confidence, so take time to examine and familiarize yourself. Don't neglect or ignore your body. The origin of sexual pleasure starts with you. Stay connected and give your body the absolute time and attention it deserves. *Learn to love and appreciate all of you.*

> "I can't imagine my life without the beauty and grace that belly dancing offers to my soul. It has been passed down to me from my mother, and now I share the same sense of history with my daughter. It's a part of her ancestors. We dance together to share each other's strength and celebrate the beauty of all women. We dance to live, and we live to dance and keep our inner siren alive."
>
> —Suhaila, Belly dancing legend

SEXUAL EMPOWERMENT.

We have been so conditioned to stay in our comfort zone, particularly when it comes to our sex life. Sexual desire is natural and the sexual fears or attitudes that you carry don't have to define or limit you. It's not disrespectful to reevaluate or explore who you are as a sexual being. In fact, it's a necessary step to being healthy and whole.

So go ahead and stay open to the possibilities around you. Sign up for a belly dancing class or doll up now and then and wear something you never thought you could. *Stepping out of your comfort zone can add a new and exciting dimension to your sex life and confidence.*

REMEMBER.

Find something tangible that moves the woman inside you, something that makes your inner siren churn. It can be a picture, a sculpture, bright red lipstick, a steamy calendar or a pair of lace stockings. Or it can be as simple as a heart attached to your key ring. Just find something that makes you feel sexy and whole, something that reminds you that you are a woman. Make sure this object is visible to you every day. Whether it's on your desk or your dresser, find a spot for it and every time you see it be reminded of your desires and desirability as a woman.

REFLECTIONS

- Who is your inner siren? When was the last time you did something to celebrate her?

- Are you comfortable with your sexuality? Why or why not?

- How do you think your life would change if you let your full femininity shine?

COMMITMENTS

- Commit to unleashing your inner siren, your sexual power.

- Commit to really knowing, learning, and loving your body.

- Commit to doing something out of your comfort zone.

CHAPTER 7

"My husband's idea of rough sex

is when I don't shave my legs."

—**Stephanie Blum, Comedienne**

CHAPTER 7

MAKE PLAYTIME!

One thing most of us forget to do is take time to work on our marriage or relationship, especially when we're busy fighting the daily demands of motherhood. Just as we send the kids into their discipline "time-out" zone, we need to carve out a special "playtime" to nurture our relationship with our significant other. Despite the demands of the day, there are many things you can do to access your seductress side and nurture your marriage or relationship.

CREATE A SACRED SPACE.

As moms, our homes are ridden with toy trucks and Barbie dolls. That's why it's so important for you to keep your bedroom private. It's crucial to create a bedroom that's sensual, inviting, and spiritually uplifting. This involves more than just a lock on the door, although that is a must! Your bedroom is your

"Your bedroom should be a warm sanctuary inspired by love and romance, a place to honor your own presence."

—Melonie Esformes, Interior designer

special place for sleeping together and making love. Creating a sacred space can be as easy as keeping the toys out and keeping candles or flowers by the bed.

FANTASIZE AND SURPRISE.

Fantasizing and surprising one another can cement bonds and create deeper intimacy. I know it seems impossible to be flirty with the kids always around, but it only takes a minute to write an enticing note or to leave a sultry message on his phone or on his nightstand. *Arousal and intimacy begin in the mind and anticipation is a huge turn on.* It's not as hard as you think. Little things really do mean a lot. So try sending him a sexy card in the mail. Write a love note and hide it in the book he's reading. Call him on the phone and sing a silly love song. Make up the words. Sing out of tune. It only takes a few minutes and it will definitely put a smile on his face. Spritz just a tiny bit of your fragrance on his briefcase so he has the scent of you all day. Use your lipstick and leave him a message on the mirror. Flash him a sweet and sexy smile when he least expects it or just flash him for fun. Igniting the passions is as easy as touching his arm affectionately when you

> "Dating your man is a great way to keep it HOT! Dinners at new spots or just meeting for a drink before you go home to the kids can keep the desire alive."
>
> —Keisha Whitaker, Wife of Forrest Whitaker

walk by or giving him a quick pat on the butt. Get creative! Come up with special code words for "I want you!" for when the kids, your friends or your parents are around. Instead of a peck on the cheek, surprise him with a sensual kiss—it can change the course of an entire day. It's the little things that will help build intimacy and ignite passion.

> "Know that sex involves your mind (what you think), your emotions (what you feel), your body image (what you perceive about yourself), your body's actions (what you do), your energy (how much energy you have to be sexual and how you move your energies within your body and between you and your partner), and your spirit (the essence of you, your spiritual path such as tantra or using sex as a pathway to the divine)."
>
> —Dr. Patti Britton, Clinical sexologist

HOT MOMS HAVE GREAT SEX!

When you are confident, empowered and your inner siren is tended to, you will naturally feel desirable and create natural desire. The more confidence you possess, the easier it will be to cultivate a passionate and fulfilling sex life.

Sex is the act of giving oneself; body, mind and spirit. A healthy sex life directly affects your family and can increase your overall energy and vitality. It's no secret that sexually satisfied people are happier and more optimistic. Hot Moms find ways to exercise their sensuality and passion regularly. Why? Because a night of great sex and real intimacy can transform your mood throughout an entire day or week.

If you've digested and incorporated the tips in the other chapters, being a siren in bed will be inevitable. Confidence in yourself, your body and your abilities will help you surrender to the moment and let go of your inhibitions and insecurities, creating greater connectedness and intimacy. And just as it's important to have confidence in your self and know what pleases you, it's just as important to know what pleases your lover. So take the time to really discover and enjoy one another.

SPICE IT UP!

Finding new and interesting places to make love will definitely spice things up. Try checking into a hotel in town and use fake names just for the thrill of it. Even the floor of the guest bedroom adds excitement and spontaneity. Explore and try new positions. I highly doubt you've DONE IT ALL! Take a bath together. Revisit the first place you met, the first place you kissed. Play footsy under the table or camp outside in your backyard. Plan an at-home date with dinner and dancing and make formal attire required. When he's on a business trip, sneak a flirty note in his bag or surprise him with a sexy wake-up call. *Be constantly looking for new and exciting ways to connect and create intimacy and passion.* It is up to you to keep that spark alive. It's okay if you have a minivan, just make it rock now and then!

> "People have asked how we keep sex creative. Willingness to be creative in the first place is half the battle. We are open and honest and we love to have fun with one another. There is nothing 'uptight' about anything that we do."
>
> —Andrea Frank Henkart, Married twenty-six years

NO EXCUSES.

Claim the nights as grown-up time. Except for special occasions, my son is in bed no later than 8:30pm without fail. It's for his good, and my sanity. The nights are mine.

Check your schedule and see where you can reorganize to fit in more "playtime." If it means waking up a half-hour earlier just to have private time together, do it. If it means putting the kids to bed a half-hour earlier, do it. Quit finding reasons or excuses why you can't or don't have the time. Here are a few reasons why you can:

- The sleepover is NOT at your house

- The kids are at your mom's

- It's date night

- You just hit rewind on *Finding Nemo*

- You've still got *it*

- Because he still turns you on

- "Everybody Loves Raymond" is a rerun

- Your child is at soccer practice for an hour

- Your newfound confidence turns him on more than ever

Hot Moms ALWAYS make time to do the things we really want to do, to do the things that feed our mind, body and spirit. Hot Moms take responsibility for their sex life. If your sex life is suffering, ask yourself why. You have the power to change it. Sex isn't dirty, bad or wrong. It's one of the most beautiful

> "We still have sex and go dancing every Saturday night!"
>
> **—Moselle Amron, Married for over sixty years!**

things we're given and it can be a very powerful force in your life. And like it or not, *you are the primary sexual educator of your children.* Their future relationships will model yours. That is why is it so important for you to have a strong sense of yourself and create solid, happy and healthy relationships.

For all you single moms out there, make time to date and meet new people. Keep a positive outlook. When I first started dating as a single mom, I was filled with insecurities. I was embarrassed and sometimes afraid to mention that I had a child. But the truth is, my son is one of the greatest things about me. If I was patient before, I am even more patient now. If was giving before, I have so much more to give now. And if I was loving before, my heart has a much larger capacity for love now. I no longer apologize for being a mom. In fact, it's the first thing I tell someone new. I have never been more proud or more excited about being a mom than now.

There's no doubt that dating as a single mother has its challenges. It's a role not every man can or wants to step in to. And that's okay. The way I see it, it takes a special man to date a mom, and I know I deserve a special man. My son is my insurance that I end up with someone special and amazing. So, go out there with a healthy sense of self and the confidence of all you have to offer and all that you deserve. In no time, you are sure to attract exactly what you are looking for. Really know and believe that!

REFLECTIONS

- Are you happy with your sex life?

_____

_____

_____

- Married or single, when was the last time you went on a date or had some "playtime"?

_____

_____

_____

- How can you create more intimacy and spice in your life?

_____

_____

_____

COMMITMENTS

- Commit to making your bedroom a sacred space (no toys allowed!).

- Commit to creating and keeping passion alive in your relationship.

- Commit to making a rockin' sex life a priority!

CHAPTER 8

"With four young children to guide through life, I have made it my lifelong promise to myself and to my children to be forever their encourager, to embrace their creativity and fill their lives with all the love their hearts can hold."

—Holly Robinson Peete, Actress and co-founder of the Hollyrod Foundation

CHAPTER 8

LOVE YOUR KIDS! LOVE YOUR LIFE!

Enthusiasm:

from the Greek word

Entheos

meaning

"Filled with the Divine"

ENJOY THE MOMENT.

Love your kids! Love your life! Duh, right? You'd be surprised how many moms I know who are so lost in the routine they forget to really enjoy the moment. I was one of them.

Last year during an unusually rainy day in Los Angeles, my son and I were out running a laundry list of errands, sprinting from the car to the store and back again. We were trying desperately not to get wet. Any time he was tempted by a puddle, I'd instinctively pull him back telling him to watch his shoes or pants.

At the next stop on my to-do list, I saw a mother carefully navigating her child around the puddles the same way I had been. It made me pause and think, "When did I get so responsible?" I then tossed my purse in the car, grabbed my son's hand and stomped right into a puddle, creating a huge splash! He laughed and shot me the "sure it's okay?" look. I nodded "yes" and I can't describe the look of joy on his face as he tore into that muddy puddle of water. We jumped and laughed and pounded the puddles until we were soaked. It was so much fun, such a tremendous release. For those brief ten minutes I didn't give an ounce of attention to what I had to do or where I had to go. I was wrapped up in the moment, living the excitement with him.

> "Until you are ready to look foolish, you'll never have the possibility of being great."
>
> —Cher, Singer and actress

I didn't get to the dry cleaners, the bank, or the post office that day. In fact, I had to add getting the car washed as well as an extra load of laundry to my to-do to list. But as I tucked my son in bed that night and told him how much fun I had with him, he looked at me with such love and said, "I hope it rains tomorrow Mom so *you* can jump in the puddles again."

Of course it's not always practical, but every once in a while we have to allow love to pull us into the moment. We need to let the moment be bigger than the errands on our list. It's easy to forget, but every moment is an opportunity to create a lasting memory with your child.

"Motherhood has, ironically, slowed me down. So many times I think everyone catches themselves worrying about doing everything right, looking good, being successful at their career, the list goes on. It all seems like a big race sometimes, but to where and for what I am not sure. But then, it is in just one moment that I catch a smile on my daughter's face. You know the kind—she just stares into your eyes and suddenly the moment stands still. It is in moments such as these that we realize we all have this intrinsic ability to be amazed and contented with the world—just as our children do—if, we can just get ourselves to...slow...down."

—Jen Mahoney, My best friend from college

"One usual day of getting the kids dressed to go some where, packing the diaper bag, buckling

> them in the car and thinking of a hundred different things, my five-year-old son asked me a question. Busy, I replied a short, 'I don't know,' to which he said, 'But Mommy, you know EVERYTHING.' It was as if a ray of light burst out of the sky and shined down on me...THE ALL KNOWING ONE! I had to laugh. I smiled and said, 'You're right, I do know everything'. We can't ruin our children's perception of us now can we?"
>
> —Joy Tilk Bergin, Co-Founder of the Hot Moms Club

SMILE!

Think about all the blessings in your life and smile. Your children should always remember you smiling. No matter how hectic the day or week has been, try to remember that every minute is precious and fleeting and attitudes are contagious. In the midst of the madness, don't forget this simple tip. Trust me, it changes everything.

Choose to be happy and let your face show it. If you have been applying the other tips, then smiling should come naturally. Remember, you are never more beautiful then when you are smiling. Create a lasting presence and know that your smile can light up a room.

One of my favorite things is my son's smile the minute he sees me after school. If it affects me that much, I can only imagine the affect my smile has on him. So make smiling a habit. Smile at your children playing. Smile at those teenagers that can't keep their hands off each other. Smile because you still feel that way about your man. Smile at the construction workers checking you out. Smile because you are well over the drinking age and you still get carded. Smile when your son throws up in your bed. Smile because it had to be the day you washed your sheets! Smile when someone asks if you are the babysitter. Smile at their face when you reply, "No, and I have one more at home twice his age!"

Guard your sense of humor with your life and remember the more you smile, the more your children will smile. Your attitude can be infectious and affect everyone around you.

LIGHTEN UP AND BE SILLY!

Once a week my son and I dance. I throw on a fun CD and we get totally goofy. We jump around and I'll do funny dance moves and he'll imitate me. Then he'll bust into a crazy move and I'll imitate him. We laugh and laugh.

By being free, by living each second and enjoying the music, the uninhibited you will build your children's

confidence and help them to laugh at themselves. Make being silly a treat but be sure to make it happen. As much joy as it brings your child, it will fill your spirit even more. As a child you had a rich imagination, so find ways to lighten up and be silly and tap in to your creativity again!

GROW YOUNG!

Your kids are your excuse to stay in touch with the kid inside of you so grow young and swing on the swings with your kids. Jump rope. Surprise them by sliding down the slide or doing a canon ball into the pool. Start a pillow fight or beep your horn like mad every time you go through a tunnel. Do whatever it is that helps you connect a piece of your childhood to theirs.

A Hot Mom is in touch with her silly side and her inner child. Whether it's singing in the shower or belting out a little Faith Hill at the top of your lungs, a Hot Mom knows how to have fun. *Invite more laughter and playfulness into your life.* And while being firm with your kids when you need to is necessary, be sure your kids see the lighter, sillier side of you.

> "You've grown up, but you haven't grown old."
>
> —**Keki Mingus, Editor and Creator of *Violet* magazine**

"One of the most important things we can give our children and ultimately ourselves as mothers is permission to have adventures. This doesn't have to be anything exotic like cliff diving; to children even the ordinary can be extraordinary.

When my children were young I could have driven them to and from school, but that would have deprived them of the fun of gaining some independence and experiencing the change of seasons and puddle jumping! Seeing the look of accomplishment on your child's face when they come home from school after walking in the rain or snow is well worth the cleanup. Hopefully it will bring back happy childhood memories. So live on the edge. Let your kids play hookie. Go to the beach or take a hike (they need mental health days too). Finger paint with chocolate pudding or lie down in a field and star gaze. By doing fun things, you will connect with your children and your inner child."

—Gail Lahm, My mom

NICKNAMES.

Snoosh, my little snooshy. I have no idea when or how I started to call my son Snoosh, but it has become my silly nickname for him and it always makes him laugh. If you don't have one already, come up with a geeky nickname for your children, something special for you and them. Make up a silly word, something funny and endearing.

PLAN A HOT DATE WITH YOUR KIDS.

Another fun thing you must do as a Hot Mom is to create a special day just for you and your child (and not their birthday). I have a special day. It's called Gabe and Mommy Day. I let my son pick the date and every year this is our special Gabe and Mommy Day. It's just for the two of us. It is a priority over everything else. Although he's too young to appreciate or really understand the importance of it, I want him to have as many incredible, magical memories and traditions with me as possible. And it's not just for him, it's for me too.

> "The best part about being a Hot Mom is throwing on my favorite jeans and heels and getting ready for a dinner date with the loves of my life—my children!"
>
> —Niki Taylor, Model

While your children may outgrow little nicknames, your special day can endure. It is never too late to create goofy traditions or create memories. Make arrangements in advance so together you can plan something fun that fits their interests. Think about the last time you had a magical moment with your child. Now think about when and how you can create one today. *Magic is free and limited only by your imagination.*

CREATE MAGIC.

It's amazing how little things can create excitement. Instead of eating at the table tonight, set up a blanket in the living room and have a picnic. It is incredible how this little change can make the meal more fun and even taste better. Serve breakfast for dinner one night. Campout in your living room as a family every now and then. Arm your kids with flashlights and spend the night telling stories. Play dress up and wear costumes even when it's not Halloween. Color a picture together or write a song. Share a secret and create fun little traditions. The more magic and creativity you foster in your own life, the more magic and creativity you can bring to your children. It's never too late. You can't give what you don't have. The magic starts in you.

"Go and run wild with your kids and capture those magic moments that often get lost and neglected due to stress and fatigue. Save the world another day."

—**Tracey Mallett, Fitness expert**

> "Make sure that your children have a packed lifetime of memories with you. Your relationship with your children is the first one they have and it will set the foundation for all of their future relationships. So no matter what your personal obstacles are or how many hours you must work in a day to get by, find time to talk to your kids, teach your kids, and just be with your kids. That is the fun part!"
>
> —Nisha Brown McClaren,
> Founder of Nisha's Little Buddies

A WORLD FILLED WITH TREASURE.

Theme parks and arcades are a huge source of amusement for our children, but don't forget about the everyday treasures that surround you. Gabe and I often take our flashlights to the park and hunt for treasures. He gets just as excited about finding a monster pine cone as he does

> "Hot Moms are committed to showing their children how many opportunities they have if they just reach out for them."
>
> —Lyss Stern, Founder of Divalyssicious Moms

about receiving a new toy. Bury random household items in the backyard for a true treasure hunt or drop change where your children can find it.

The world is filled with treasures. We have to open ourselves and our children up to all of the wonder that surrounds us daily. Create a treasure box and fill it with all that you find, your memories from special days.

"I love flowers and so does my little girl, Maddy. When she was first learning to walk we would go through the neighborhood picking wild flowers. We would talk about how beautiful they were, what colors they were, their names. Then one day I saw her looking at me curiously every time I would put a flower to my nose. She didn't know what I was doing. So I proceeded to teach her how to 'smell the roses.' It ain't that easy folks! The words *inhale* and *exhale* don't have much meaning at this point. For the next few months, every time I would give Maddy a flower she would smile, put it to her nose and blow snot all over it. Some laughs last forever. Write them down!"

—Brooke Burns, Actress

REFLECTIONS

- What are some of your favorite childhood memories? How can you recreate them for your children?

  _____

  _____

  _____

- What was the silliest thing you recently did, on purpose?

  _____

  _____

  _____

- What magical moment did you share with your kids this week?

  _____

  _____

  _____

COMMITMENTS

- Commit to letting you inner child out, to loving your life and living right now, in this moment.

- Commit to planning a hot date with your kids.

- Commit to building a treasure box and filling it with wondrous memories.

THE HOT MOM'S OATH

Read it. Say it. Repeat it. Frame it. And most importantly, LIVE IT!

I, Hot Mom _____, recognize that motherhood broadens and expands me. For the sake of

_____

(name your children), I will foster my spirit, my dreams and my inner light. I will be kind to myself and love who I am. I will let go of all negativity, regrets, doubts and fears. I will take time for me, guilt free. I say it again, GUILT FREE! I will find a way to rejuvenate myself when I am stressed. I will make room for intimacy and create healthy relationships in my life. I will release my inner goddess and let my children see the fun and silly side of me at least once a week. I will live in the moment and I will really know and understand that being good to myself is the greatest gift I can give my children. It may take some time, but I am committed and strong. When I find my center and my balance, I will help other moms do the same.

- In addition, I will wear an outrageous pair of underwear to _____ at *least* once a year.

- I will surprise my significant other with _____ at *least* once a month.

- I will treat myself to_____ at *least* once a week.

- I will rejoice in myself at *least* once a day!

Sign _____

Date _____

WORDS OF WISDOM

I'm not Supermom. I know I'm not perfect—far from it—and actually, I don't try to be. One of the most important lessons I've learned over the past eighteen years is that not only is it impossible to be Supermom, I don't want to be.

I am important, as a woman and an individual, not simply as a mother and wife. I've learned that if a woman gives up one aspect of herself—the woman in her, the mother, or the wife—the other facets suffer. Often women think the opposite: that if they just concentrate on being good mothers (preferably, perfect mothers) then they'll automatically be good women and wives. Nothing could be further from the truth. A woman must be aware of herself and her needs so she can be aware of the needs of her family. Women don't need to feel guilty about taking care of themselves, because it will only help them do a better job of caring for others. You must take care of yourself first for everyone else's sake, as well as for your own.

You owe it to yourself to focus on finding the way to your own heart. I believe that every woman regardless of how many roles she juggles not only has the power to be in control of her life but has the innate ability to pull it all off with great aplomb and joy.

—Kathryn Sansone, Author of *Woman First, Family Always* (©2006, Meredith Books) and happily-married mother of 10

EPILOGUE

"Every mom has a situation they handle successfully that could help or inspire others."

—**Linda Swain, Host and creator of Moms On the Move**

"There's comfort in numbers and power in girlfriends."

—Miami Bombshells, Authors of *Dish & Tell: Life, Love and Secrets*

FLAUNT YOURSELF AND YOUR NEW ATTITUDE.

Being a Hot Mom is an awesome state of mind and outlook. This is a movement. There is strength in numbers. Spread your light and share these secrets with other moms. Encourage and inspire all of the moms you know to be and feel HOT! Start a Hot Moms Club in your area and learn to lean on each other. If you've already got a moms group, rename yourselves the Hot Moms Club. It's funny how people actually become their labels.

The Hot Moms Club was born out of my own need to feel confident as a single mom. Surrounding myself with remarkable, inspiring moms helped me overcome my insecurities. I constantly drew and still draw from their strengths and experiences. Fill your world with incredible mothers. Open yourself to all moms. The moment you close yourself off to anyone or anything, you limit your ability to grow. Hot Moms recognize the importance of who they are, their friendships, and the power they posess. Share what you've learned.

"It takes love, support, and dedication beyond what you could ever have expected to be a great parent. And guess what? You can do it. You can love it. And you can always ask for help. I encourage all of you to reach out and assist one another in being super parents. Start a Hot Moms Club in your community today!"

—Nisha Brown McClaren,
Founder of Nisha's Little Buddies

ACKNOWLEDGEMENTS

I'd like to acknowledge Joy Tilk Bergin, Karma Mc-Cain and Kristen Jarin for their dedication in the midst of mothering, family and career; their unwavering commitment and energy have made this vision a reality.

With much love I thank the amazing people in my life, my friends who have helped move H.M.C. forward. I am forever touched and grateful to Marcus Dell, Bruce Martin, Craig Andujar, Jeff Alholm, Janet Gunn, Meredith Brooks, Keisha Whitaker, Ira Kurgan, Rachel Hill, Roshni Lata Mangal, Sharon Segal, Nina Segal, Carrie Stevens, Brooke Burns, Angie DeGrazia, Lesa Amoore, Natasha Henstridge, Tara Sebastiano, Christina Harrison, Angie Degrazia, Kara Chaput, Jesse Kirshner, Janelle Paradee, Melonie Esformes, Chris Georges, Nisha Brown-McClaren, Marianne Stanley, Karen McCain, Bryan Dattilo, Mo, Jordan Schelcter, and B.

Special thanks to Warren Kohler for his remarkable business sense, master organizing skills and generous heart.

With all of my heart I would like to thank my family, Mom, Dad, Kim, Jeffrey, Jenn, and Grandma. Thank you for your unconditional understanding, patience and help. I love you guys!

Warmest wishes to all of the extraordinary moms that have contributed to this book and all of the incredible moms who contribute to the website. You inspire me with your wisdom and sense of humor.

Thank you to my agent Michael Broussard for believing in this and in me. Shout out to Nena and Jennifer at Dupree Miller.

Thank you, thank you, thank you, to David Dunham and the entire Thomas Nelson team. You have made this experience a blast!

This book would not exist without my incredible editor and friend Rebekah Whitlock. You have made this process an absolute joy. Thank you for your guidance, wisdom and notes of encouragement. You are an inspiration. The Hot Moms Club is both honored and excited to be a part of your vision and hot new imprint, NAKED INK!

ABOUT JESSICA DENAY

Jessica Denay is a single mom, determined to redefine the traditional image of motherhood. To help other moms find confidence and a community of resources, she and her friends began HMCmagazine.com. The stage was set and the movement was born, right out of her living room!

Jessica is a former teacher and counselor from New "Joisey." She lives in Los Angeles with her son Gabriel. She loves avocados, hot tea, a great book, acoustic music and goofing around with her "little man" at the beach. Her children's book series will be out next year and she has a script moving into production this summer. She has recently gotten to level five in Ms. Pac man.

For more information about Jessica and the Hot Moms Club visit www.HMCmagazine.com and www.HaveMoreCompassion.org

ABOUT THE HOT MOMS WHO CONTRIBUTED

The Hot Moms Club thrives on the bond of motherhood. It's supporting and learning from each other. It's friendship and it's community. It was only natural to fill this handbook with quotes, stories and wisdom from some of the most remarkable moms I know. Here is a little more about the moms in this book.

Beth Aldrich—Chicago based mother of three boys, Beth is creator and founder of *For Her Information*, a television show and magazine. She is devoted to women's issues and the environment. Please visit www.forherinformation.com.

Rasheda Ali—Mother of two boys, Rasheda is the daughter of Mohamed Ali. She wrote *I'll Hold Your Hand So You Won't Fall: A Child's Guide to Parkinson's Disease,* a book which communicates to children the difficulties faced by those who suffer from Parkinson's disease.

Moselle Amron—Eighty-one-year-old mother of two, Moselle is a championship dancer. She entertained the American and British troops during the war. She is in a loving, passionate marriage of sixty years.

Elizabeth Blanchard—Yoga instructor who continues to teach and practice yoga in her eighth month of pregnancy. She is the wife of yoga guru Mark Blanchard. Please visit www.markblanchardpoweryoga.com.

Stephanie Blum—Mother of two and 'apathetic mom next door' whose trademark laziness and procrastination is sarcastic, hilarious and universally adored by audiences. A Brooklyn native and former school psychologist, she became addicted to writing and performing comedy after winning New York's Funniest Teacher contest. Stephanie has won many other comedy competitions including Star Search and the 2002 Ladies of Laughter Funniest Female at Madison Square Garden. Please visit www.stephanieblum.com.

Kailynn Bowling—Mommy to one toddler boy, Kailynn is co-founder of Chicblvd.com, a "chic" resource for the road of life which includes guidelines for dating, weddings, baby and living, all from a modern day perspective. Please visit www.chicblvd.com.

Alicia Brandt—Mom of two girls and co-founder of Women's Night Out, a monthly show for and about women. Please visit www.womensnightout.info.

Dr. Patti Britton—Known as "Dr. Patti" she is a nationally board-certified Clinical Sexologist/Sex Coach, frequent media guest, President-Elect of the American Association of Sexuality Educators, Counselors and Therapists as well as popular workshop leader & speaker. She is author of *The Art of Sex Coaching, The Complete Idiot's Guide to Sensual Massage* and *The Adventures of Her in France*. Please visit www.yoursexcoach.com.

Meredith Brooks—Multi-platinum, Grammy-nominated recording artist who has also produced and written records for some of today's hottest stars. Recently, Meredith has turned her creative energy and passion to writing and recording her latest children's record and producing music and concerts for families. Please visit www.meredithbrooks.com.

Brooke Burns—Actress and mom of one little girl, Brooke has an amazing spirit and an ever-positive attitude. Her laugh, smile, and energy light up a room.

Daniella Clark—Known as the Master of Denim, Daniella is widely credited for starting the rage of the now-standard, low-rise jeans with her Frankie-B's.

Nancy Cleary—Mom of two, Nancy is an advocate for work-at-home moms. Her publishing company Wyatt-MacKenzie Publishing Inc. is named for her two children. For seven years she has brought the ideas of mom writers and entrepreneurs to fruition. She created and publishes the only mom's business magazine. Please visit www.wymacpublishing.com.

Chani Demello—Mom of two boys, Chani is the founder of Moms on Boards. She is a surfer mom whose mission is to honor, celebrate, recognize, represent, and encourage moms of all walks of life to live proud and find the one thing which nurtures the spirit and frees the soul. Please visit www.momsonboards.com.

Melonie Esformes—A mom of two beautiful little girls, Melonie is a sought after Hollywood interior designer with impeccable taste and style.

Tricia Leigh Fisher—Single mom of one, Tricia created Nana's Garden along with her sister Joely Fisher and mother Connie Stevens. Nana's Garden is a magical place where moms can catch up with friends, get a pedicure, and their kids can play within eye shot. Please visit www.nanasgarden.net.

Chris Georges—Single mom of one grown daughter, Chris is a private chef and develops recipes for Whole Foods®.

Anna Getty—Member of the distinguished Getty family, Anna is a writer, producer, yoga teacher and mother of one. She is also the creator of *The Divine Mother Prenatal Yoga Series* DVD. Please visit www.annagetty.com.

Kathie Lee Gifford—Mom of two children, Cody and Cassidy, Kathie is a playwright, singer, songwriter and producer. She is best known as the former co-host of "LIVE with Regis & Kathie Lee." In her fifteen years on the show, Gifford received nine Emmy® nominations. After a five-year absence, she is now a special correspondent for "The Insider." Gifford devotes much of her time to the Association to Benefit Children, which spawned the Cody Foundation. The resources from the Association continue to support Cody House and Cassidy's Place. Cody House provides a transitional home for infants and children who have severe disabilities and serious medical problems. Named for Gifford's daughter, Cassidy's Place is the home of the Association to Benefit Children's (ABC) national children advocacy. Gifford is the Celebrity Spokeswoman for the National Children's Advocacy Center, which works to prevent and educate against the physical and sexual abuse of children. Please visit www.kathieleegifford.com.

Janet Gunn—Actress and sought after jewelry designer, Janet is the proud mom of one little boy, Luca.

Andrea Frank Henkart—Psy.D. and mother of two, Andrea is an international parenting expert, motivational speaker, and acclaimed author of five books on childbirth, family communication, and health and nutrition for parents and kids. She has taught over tenthousand kids in her babysitter seminars nationwide.

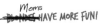

Featured on *Oprah* in addition to hundreds of other TV and radio shows, Andrea and her daughter, Journey, are the only mother-daughter team that travel, write books together and give seminars around the globe. Please visit www.coolcommunication.com.

Lauren Holly—Mother of three boys, Lauren is an incredible actress whose extensive feature film credits include "Dumb and Dumber," "What Women Want," "No Looking Back," "Any Given Sunday," "Sabrina," "Turbulence," "Beautiful Girls," "Dragon: The Bruce Lee Story," and many more! Her upcoming films include "Fatwa," for which she additionally serves as executive producer, "Godfather of Green Bay," "The Chumscrubber," and "Pleasure Drivers." Holly was born in Bristol, Pennsylvania and attended Sarah Lawrence College. She currently lives in Chicago, Ill. with her husband and her sons. Look for Lauren as she returns to television as NCIS Director Jenny Shepard on CBS's top-rated drama series "NCIS."

Sheila Kelly—Mother of two, Sheila is the founder of the extraordinary movement called Sfactor. She combined a great workout with an inspiring body attitude and turned it into a worldwide trend. Her striptease and pole dancing workouts empower women everywhere. Please visit www.sfactor.com.

Rochelle L'Italien—Registered dietitian and single mom of two boys (who regularly read nutrition labels and sort food groups at the dinner table!), her hobby of riding freestyle BMX on jumps and ramps feeds her spiritual appetite. She took up this hobby at age thirty-seven and calls it her moving meditation. See her rider profile at www.wofbmx.com.

Gail Lahm—My mom, a mother of three, and a no-nonsense Italian from Jersey who is fifty-five (but easily looks ten years younger). She coaches crew and makes the best pasta fagioli. She was a nurse, my girl scout leader, and will always be my hero.

Diana Lang—A spiritual counselor and yoga teacher since 1980, Diana is the author of *Opening to Meditation*. She holds conventions on body awareness, stress reduction, and mind/body workouts. Please visit www.dianalang.com.

Jennifer Nicole Lee—After the birth of her second son, Jennifer lost 70 pounds leading her to be crowned Ms. Bikini America and the 1st ever Ms. Muscle and Fitness. She enjoys being a Hot Mom and helping other women achieve their fitness goals with her book *Crack the Code: Unlock Your Fat Burning & Weight Loss Potential* and her line of exercise DVDs. To learn more about this incredible modern day weight loss success story and fitness model, please visit www.jennifernicolelee.com.

—— ✂ ——

Jeanine Lobell—Mother of four, Jeanine is one of the most renowned make-up artists in the business and the creator of Stila cosmetics. Stila has sponsored our makeover events for homeless and abused mothers by generously donating awesome products and makeup artists. Please visit www.stilacosmetics.com.

Jennifer Mahoney—A mother of one with another on the way, she is my best friend since college and my soul mate in a woman. Although more than 3,000 miles away, she's my cherished friend.

Tracey Mallett—Mom of two, Fitness Expert & Master Trainer for over fifteen years. Popular host of *The Method Show* and DVDs and creator of a new fitness series designed for the Hot Mom called "3 in 1 Patented Pregnancy System" and "Super Body Boot Camp." Tracey's mission is to motivate moms to find time to exercise and ultimately reach their goals! Please visit www.traceymallett.com and www.atptraining.com.

Cindy Margolis—Mother of three, Cindy is a supermodel, actress, author, and the spokesperson for

RESOLVE: The National Infertility Association. Please visit www.cindymargolis.com.

Karma McCain—Mother of one little boy, Karma is a co-founder of the Hot Moms Club. A complex, beautiful spirit, she directs and runs our charity **H**ave **M**ore **C**ompassion. Please visit www.havemorecompassion.org.

Nisha Brown McClaren—Proud mom of two daughters, she is the founder of Nisha's Little Buddies. She educates children with her training organization Devoted to Making a Difference in Quality Childcare and Parenting. She is currently planning dates for her popular workshop series. Please visit www.nishaslittlebuddies.com.

Eve Michaels—Mom of three and step-mother of two, Eve is an image consultant who has dedicated her life to helping moms get their WOW back! Please visit www.evemichaels.com.

Dr. Evelyn Budd Michaels—Mother of one grown son, Evelyn has a PhD in Psychology. She is a counselor with over twenty-five years experience in assisting people with personal growth and development. She has reached millions of people throughout the world via TV, radio, and seminars. She produced and hosted the cable television show *Synergy 4 Success.*

Keki Mingus—The editor-in-chief and creator of *Violet*, a magazine for modern family living. Please visit www.violetmagazine.com.

Holly Robinson Peete—Super mom of four, Holly is an actress, author, and philanthropist. With her husband, she founded the Hollyrod Foundation dedicated to providing medical, physical, and emotional support to those suffering from Parkinson's disease. Please visit www.hollyrod.org.

Chynna Phillips—A mom of three, singer, and songwriter.

Kelly Preston—Involved and dedicated mom of two, Kelly is an actress, humanitarian and a prominent activist for parents and children's rights. Please visit www.fightforkids.org.

Joy Rose—Founder of MAMAPALOOZA, Joy is motivated to create opportunities for other mom performers. Joy hosted the first underground Mamapalooza at the Cutting Room in NYC with cookie jar money. She is also the founder and lead singer of the rock band, House Wives On Prozac. Please visit www.mamapalooza.com.

Sara Rosenberg—Mom of two and one of the six Miami Bombshells who authored the *Dish & Tell: Life, Love and Secrets.* To be a bombshell all you need is a dose of spice, a little sex appeal, a dash of soul, and the desire to embrace every inch of yourself. Please visit www.miamibombshells.com

Carmen Richardson Rutlen—Author of the book *Dancing Naked...in fuzzy red slippers* which was awarded The Benjamin Franklin Award in 2005 as well as the BAIPA Book Award for Best in Humor and Inspiration. Carmen is working on her second book and still considers her self a Hot Mom (and she's not talking about hot flashes!).

Lyss Stern—Mother of one little boy. I love her voice, her energy, her boldness. She is the founder of the popular Divalysscious Moms where she coordinates incredible events for mothers and their kids in NYC. Please visit www.divalyssciousmoms.com.

Linda Swain—Mom of six, Linda hosts and produces *Moms On the Move* where she profiles real and inspiring

moms who are making a difference in their homes and communities. Please visit www.momsonthemove.com.

Suhaila Salimpour—A mother of one and the daughter of Jamila Salimpour, Suhaila is a pioneer in the world of Middle Eastern dance. She is one of the world's most sought after performers, teachers and belly dance choreographers. Please visit www.suhaila.com.

Niki Taylor—Mom of twin boys, Niki is a supermodel, entrepreneur, designer and founder of the Begin Foundation. Please visit www.nikitaylor.com.

Joy Tilk Bergin—Mother of two, Joy is a co-founder of the Hot Moms Club. She is my rock, a loyal friend, dedicated mom, and sharp business partner, not to mention the model for our logo.

Carilyn Vaile—Mom of two, Carilyn is the author of *I Am Diva! Every Woman's Guide to Outrageous Living.* Carilyn is a successful designer of contemporary stretch knit sportswear for every woman. Please visit www.carilynvaile.com and www.iamdiva.com.

Andrea Vincent—Mom of one, Andrea is the founder of SeeMOMMYrun, a national organization that helps mothers connect and exercise together through unified programs and activities. Please visit www.seemommyrun.com.

— ❦ —

Catherine Wayland—Co-founder of *International Family Magazine,* a monthly online magazine that celebrates families worldwide and is published in English, Spanish, Korean, Indian and Chinese. Catherine is a proud mama of two beautiful boys, Jax and Brody, and is gratefully married to her best friend, John Hoffman. Please visit www.internationalfamilymag.com.

Keisha Whitaker—A mother of three girls and a bundle of energy and spunk, Keisha is the wife of Forrest Whitaker, as well as a super model and super mom. Read her popular column Keisha's Korner at www.hmcmagazine.com.

Nita Whitaker—Singer and mother of two, her new album and song *If I Had Never Known You* was inspired by her daughters. To hear the voice of an angel visit www.nitawhitaker.com

Carrie Wiatt—Renown nutritionist, mom, chef and author of *Eating by Design* and *Portion Savvy: The 30 Day Smart Plan for Eating Well* and *The Diet for Teenagers Only*. Please visit www.dietdesigns.com.

Carnie Wilson—Mother of one little girl, Carnie is a singer, author, actress, and voice-over artist.

ABOUT HAVE MORE COMPASSION

"Words of love, hugs of trust, smiles of confidence—
all mixed together with unconditional validity and infinite
perseverance creates a person with compassionate stance.
Compassion is our soul. It is our access, our connection,
our pass to being whole."

—Roshni Lata Mangal

The Hot Moms Club is dedicated to helping battered, single and struggling moms. **H**ave **M**ore **C**ompassion, based on our acronym, is the fund in which we help support moms in need. Currently we are working with Vera House and their Onward and Upward program for mothers trying to get out of abusive relationships and The Good Shepherd Shelter for moms who have survived domestic abuse, and The Good Shepherd Center for homeless and disabled mothers.

Portions of all of our merchandise sales and portions of this book's proceeds go directly to this fund.

Visit www.HaveMoreCompassion.org to find out more about what we do and how you can help.